Don't Get Screwed!

How to Protect Yourself as an Independent Musician

Erin M. Jacobson, Esq.

Indie Artist Resource

Published by:

Indie Artist Resource LLC

© 2020 Erin M. Jacobson, Esq. All Rights Reserved.

It is illegal to reproduce, duplicate, or transmit any part of this document in any format or media now known or hereafter devised.

Thank you for purchasing an authorized copy of this book. Copyright is important as it allows authors to create and enjoy the benefits of their creative works.

For Mom

Table of Contents

Disclaimer   7
About This Book   9
Introduction   11

PART I: Ownership of Musical Works   13

1. Musical Compositions and Master Recordings   14
2. Copyright and Trademark   17

PART II: Royalties and Making Money from Music   24

3. Royalties   25
4. Royalty Collection Services   31
    The Ultimate Royalty Reference Guide   38
5. Keep Your Catalogue Clean   43

PART III: Music Agreements   47

6. Contract Terms   48
7. Music Publishing Agreements   51
8. Recording Agreements   61
9. Agreements Needed for Independent Musicians   65

Conclusion	78
Notes	79
Appendix A	82
Acknowledgments	83
About the Author	85

Disclaimer

This book and its contents are provided for educational and informational purposes only. The content contained in this book is not legal advice or a legal opinion on any specific matter or matters.

This book or the information in it does not constitute or create an attorney-client relationship between Erin M. Jacobson, Esq. and you or any other reader. Throughout the book, references to the reader as "you" are solely for writing style and the ease of reading, but again, there is no legal advice being provided to you and there is no attorney-client relationship created with Erin M. Jacobson, Esq.

The law may vary based on the facts or particular circumstances or the law in your state. You should not act, or fail to act, upon this information without seeking the professional counsel of an attorney licensed in your state.

If this book or its content is considered an advertisement, it is general in nature and not directed towards any particular person or entity.

The "real world examples" provided throughout this book are all real examples, but do not list any names or identifying characteristics for confidentiality reasons.

About This Book

There are a lot of expectations in life, so I begin this book by giving you an idea of what you can expect from it.

This book is not a full textbook and it is not everything you will ever need to know in your career or in every contract. This book is a plain English, straight to the point, primer on the topics you need to understand to make important decisions about your music career.

In this book, I explain:

- what copyright really means and why you should register yours,
- the different types of royalties and how they actually apply in the real world so you can understand how and when your music earns money,
- how to get paid the royalties your music earns,
- the contracts most needed by independent musicians and why they are important,
- traps to avoid, and

- real examples of mistakes musicians have made and how you can avoid making them too.

Whether you are just starting out in your career, gaining some traction, or have been in the business for many years, this book will explain these concepts to you in a brief and direct format. Musicians have told me that they learned more in a 10-minute explanation from me than in their entire careers as working musicians[1], and I want this book to empower you with the knowledge to make informed decisions and grow your career.

Best of luck!

Introduction

I have always loved music. I've considered myself a "professional appreciator" of it. About half-way through college, I was first exposed to copyright and music contracts, and how many musicians were being taken advantage of and making poor business decisions. All of this information struck a chord (pun intended) with something inside my being, and I knew part of my mission would be to help protect music creators. That was the moment when I decided to become a music attorney.

Throughout my career, I have seen – and prevented – many scenarios where musicians were being taken advantage of, but I also found many of these instances included an element where the musician didn't understand enough to know whether he or she was signing a bad deal. Fortunately, many of these situations can be prevented with a little bit of knowledge and action, and in this book, I'll go over the real, correct information to give you a solid foundation to take steps forward in your career. This is information that many superstar musicians, or musicians that have been in the business for many years, still don't understand, so this information will be invaluable on your music career journey.

Let's get started.

PART I
Ownership of Musical Works

Chapter One
Musical Compositions and Master Recordings

An important concept in the music industry is the concept that the musical composition and the master recording of that composition are separate. Normally, when we hear a song on the radio, we think of a song as one entity.

However, from a legal and business perspective, and from an income collection standpoint, a song is not just one entity. A "song" is comprised of the musical composition, which includes the music, melody, and lyrics (i.e. what you would see on a lead sheet if you wrote out the musical notes, etc.), and the master recording, which is a sound recording of an artist's performance of a particular composition.

My favorite example to illustrate the separation between the composition and the master recording is The Beatles' song, "Yesterday." The composition was written by John Lennon and Paul McCartney[2], and the first master recording of that composition was of a performance by The Beatles. However, there is also a recording of "Yesterday" (the composition) by Elvis Presley, which is another master recording. There is another recording of "Yesterday" (the composition) by Frank Sinatra, which is another master recording. In fact, there are actually thousands of different recordings of "Yesterday," as it is one of the most covered compositions in music history. Although all of these master recordings of "Yesterday" exist, there is still only one composition. This holds true for all compositions and the various master recordings of those compositions. Therefore, it is always important to think of the separation between the musical composition and the master recording.

The composition is usually owned by either a music publisher or a songwriter depending on the songwriter's stature, and whether the songwriter has a contractual relationship with a music publisher. The master recording is usually owned by either the artist, a record label, maybe a producer, or some other company, again depending on the artist's

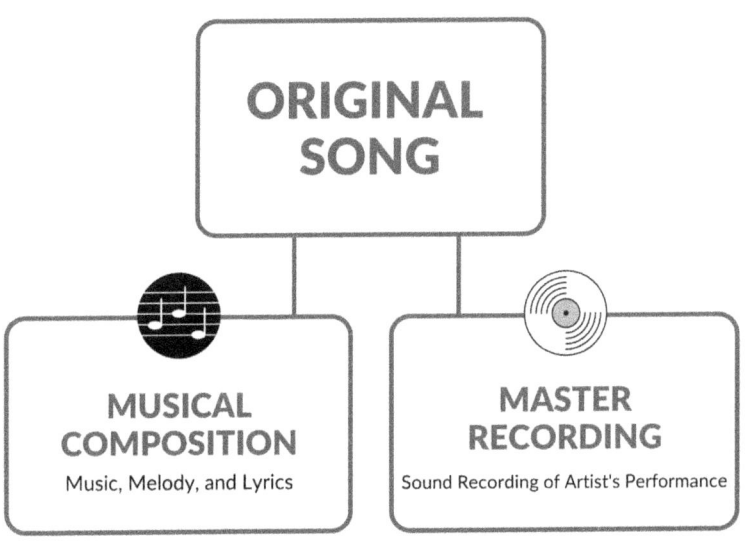

stature and what agreements the artist has made. The composition and the master recording each come with their own separate copyrights, and their own royalty streams, to be discussed shortly.

Chapter Summary

- Musical compositions are the music, melody, and lyrics.
- Master recordings are the recordings of an artist's performance of a musical composition.
- Compositions and master recordings are separate entities that each have their own copyright ownership and royalty streams.

Chapter Two
Copyright and Trademark

The moment a work is created with sufficient originality for copyright protection and is "fixed in a tangible medium of expression,"[3] that work has copyright protection. A "tangible medium of expression" means that the work is put into a physical form that can be reproduced, such as recording it or writing it on paper. One thing to note is that a title is not copyrightable.

Your next question might be "What does it mean to have a copyright?" A copyright is a limited monopoly on the ownership of a work, which means the ability to have the authority over its use and earn income from one's creative work. The current term of copyright for new works created is the length of the life of the author plus 70 years.[4]

There are a set of rights that come with every copyright which includes the rights to:

- reproduce,
- distribute,

- publicly perform,
- display (which is the equivalent of performance for visual works, like an art piece or other stationary visual medium),
- make derivative works (also called the adaptation right), and
- digitally perform the master recording.

The owner of the copyright has control over all of these uses of the work. The owner can say whether and how a work is used and can benefit from those uses monetarily.

Copyright Registration

Even though a work is protected by copyright as soon as it's "fixed in a tangible medium of expression," there are benefits to filing a federal copyright registration application through the United States Copyright Office. Those benefits include:

- Being able to sue in federal court for copyright infringement;
- A public notice of who owns the work;
- Listing in the United States Copyright Office's online databases;
- A legal presumption of ownership of the work in court (if certain conditions are met);
- Statutory damages and attorney's fees (i.e. more money!) can be awarded to the winner of an infringement suit (if certain conditions are met); and

- The date of creation listed on a federal registration certificate is the strongest evidence a court will consider.

I'll emphasize two of these benefits again:

- **A person (or company) cannot sue in federal court for copyright infringement without a registration with the U.S. Copyright Office, and**
- **The date of creation listed on a federal registration certificate is the strongest evidence a court will consider.**

A lot of people ask me about the "Poor Man's Copyright," which is when a person records his or her music on a CD or writes down the lyrics, puts it in an envelope, and mails it to himself or herself.

People think the date of the postmark serves as sufficient evidence of the date of creation for copyright protection, but it does not. A court will *only* consider the date on a federal copyright registration certificate. While having an envelope with a postmark is maybe better than having nothing, it is not something that is going to be relied on by a court as evidence of a date of creation.

In the last several years, people have also asked me, "What about when I post a video of my song on YouTube or online, because the post would have a date stamp?" The answer is still no. I've coined that example as the "Poor Man's Copyright 2.0," and it doesn't hold any more effect than mailing it to yourself in an envelope. Again, a court is *only* going to look at a federal copyright registration for a date of creation.

Recently, some companies have appeared online offering to give encrypted date stamps to show evidence of the date of creation of a work. These companies charge just a few dollars per registration and make it appear that using their service will save the user a lot of money in comparison to the fees of the U.S. Copyright Office (ranging from $45-65 per application at the time of this publication).

Here's why this is a problem: First, as already explained, **the date of creation listed on a federal registration certificate is the strongest evidence a court will consider.** While a court may look at other outside evidence, there is absolutely no guarantee they will accept this evidence, and a court will still require the federal registration certificate. When I have inquired about whether these companies have any instances of a court accepting the registrations they offer as valid, I have not received a response, and the fine print on these companies websites states there is no guarantee their registration will be accepted as evidence by a court. In other words, the answer is no.

Second, **a federal registration certificate is required to pursue a copyright infringement claim in federal court.** If one does not have a federal registration certificate and an infringement (or potential infringement) occurs, the owner of the allegedly infringed work will then have to immediately register the work with the U.S. Copyright Office in order to pursue the claim, AND will have to rush the application to pursue that claim timely. The Copyright Office calls this rushed status "Special Handling," and charges a fee of $800 (at the time of this publication) to rush the processing time for the application.

While someone thought spending less than $5 on a "registration" with a private company was saving money, that person would end up having to pay $845-865 just to obtain a federal registration to have the ability to defend an infringement for one work. If the person initially registered the work correctly with the Copyright Office, the fee would have been $45-65, and would have come with all the protections afforded by federal registration, saving that person $800 (plus the money already spent on the other "registration" company).

Again, the best way to have all benefits of copyright protection is by registering works with the U.S. Copyright Office. Artists can register for copyright protection on their own or hire an attorney to do it. Some types of works can be grouped together to save on application fees, but not all, so it's best to consult an expert attorney.

Trademark

People also often ask me about "copyrighting their band name." As mentioned earlier, titles cannot be registered for copyright or enjoy copyright protection. Further, band names fall under what is called a trademark or service mark (I'll refer to both of these collectively as trademark for ease of reading). Trademarks protect the names of brands and companies that provide goods or services in commerce. In a band context, this would mean that people know a certain band provides a certain type of music to the public and therefore anything attributed to the band's name would also create an expectation in the market (i.e. with fans or the public) of a certain quality of product, production, and/or experience. Trademark law protects these brands so that someone else cannot try to capitalize on that band's name and confuse the public. For example, if your neighbor's garage band called themselves The Rolling Stones and played a show in your neighborhood, you (and probably most everyone else who bought tickets) would be pretty upset to show up and find out that the act for the evening is actually Joe and Bobby from next door instead of Mick, Keith, Ron, and Charlie.

Trademarks can gain protection by use in the marketplace, but registering a trademark with the United States Patent and Trademark Office (USPTO) gives additional protections to a name, similar to how registering with the Copyright Office gives additional protections to the owner of a creative work. Again, one of the most important benefits here is that a person cannot sue in federal court for trademark infringement without a federal registration from the USPTO.

As discussed in relation to copyright, watch out for other "registration" companies and name databases, as they do not provide the protections they offer. Again, the best way to protect your trademark is to register with the USPTO.

Trademark registration is based on registering in different categories of good and services provided, and the fees will vary based on the number of categories registered. Musicians usually will register in one or two categories, but will sometimes register for additional categories if, for example, they also want to release merchandise.

While trademarks can be registered by an individual, the applications and requirements are very complex, and it is advised to seek an experienced attorney to handle this for you. It is also highly recommended that a professional name search is done prior to registration, otherwise, you may spend a lot of money on a trademark registration application only to be denied registration and lose your application fee. The application fees usually start about $225-275 per category for online filings (at the time of this publication). Another thing to note is that registering your mark will be a U.S. registration. There is no such thing as an "international" registration that will register your mark in all countries worldwide. Most countries in the world will recognize registered trademarks in other countries, but if for some reason you really need a mark registered in other countries, then that would be done on a country-by-country basis.

Chapter Summary

- Copyright comes with a list of rights exclusive to that copyright owner.
- Enjoy all of the benefits of copyright protection by registering works with the U.S. Copyright Office.
- Band names are protected by trademark law.
- Enjoy all of the benefits of trademark protection by registering with the U.S. Patent and Trademark Office.

PART II
Royalties and Making Money from Music

Chapter Three
Royalties

As mentioned above, in addition to having their own separate copyrights, compositions and master recordings also have their own separate royalty streams. I like to say, "there's a royalty for that," because almost every use of a composition and master recording has a royalty stream, and each of these royalty streams for both compositions and master recordings are tied to one of the rights of copyright listed in the last chapter.

Composition: Mechanical Royalties

Mechanical royalties correspond to the reproduction and distribution rights of copyright, and were named when compositions were mechanically reproduced onto audio mediums such as player piano rolls. Mechanical royalties are paid from the person/company reproducing the composition (usually the record label) to the owner of the musical composition (usually the music publisher) for the privilege of reproducing and distributing that composition on a recording. The mechanical rates for physical goods and downloads are set by the government, so you will hear that amount referred to as the "statutory rate," or "stat rate," for short. The statutory rate has varied over the years, but at the time of this writing is 9.1¢ for musical compositions five minutes or less in duration, and there are pro-rated rates for longer compositions.

There is also a mechanical royalty for interactive streaming uses (interactive meaning the listener can choose the song he or she wants to listen to, such as on Spotify) because there is a data reproduction in the stream. The rates for mechanical streaming are calculated by using a complicated formula based on many factors, such as the revenue of the streaming service, the total number of streams, whether the users were on free, ad-supported accounts, or paid subscription accounts, and more. Rates therefore can vary, but generally work out to fractions of a penny per stream, and it takes A LOT of streams to make any significant income.

Composition: Public Performance Royalties

Compositions also come with a public performance royalty. A public performance of a work is when a work is performed and capable of being heard by the public or by a substantial number of people outside one's family and friends. Note that "performed" does not mean only a live performance, it could also be the transmission of a piece of music, such as when a song is played on the radio or television, or over the speakers at a restaurant. When a composition is publicly performed on radio, television, streaming, in live performances, etc., a royalty is generated for each of those performances. Compositions do not earn public performance royalties from movie theatres in the United States, but cinemas outside the United States do pay performance royalties.

Royalties for performance are also calculated based on complicated formulas. For example, the calculation for television performances has to do with time of broadcast (i.e. primetime vs. the middle of the night), what channel it was broadcast on, whether the music was featured as a live performance, theme song, or background instrumental, and many other factors. Each type of performance has unique factors considered, as well as a weighting scale to determine the amount of royalties owed. Therefore, rates will vary.

Composition: Print Royalties

The print royalty is tied to the reproduction right of copyright, and there are print royalties for uses including sheet music and folios, and lyric reprints. This means lyrics on T-shirts, YouTube videos, and those lyric websites all should be paying royalties (although many of them don't, and that is called copyright infringement).

Composition: Synchronization Fees

Compositions also have a synchronization fee for the reproduction of the composition in an audio-visual production, such as a TV show, film, video game, internet production, etc. A synchronization fee is a contractual fee agreed upon between the production and the composition owner (usually the music publisher) to synchronize the composition with the visual elements in that audio-visual production. Again, while it's not a royalty, synchronization, or "sync" income is a large part of the income collected for compositions.

Master Royalties

Master recordings are owned by a record label, or artist, or maybe another company to which the artist has assigned ownership of the masters. The most typical master recording royalties are for sales, which occurs when physical product like a CD or a digital project like a download is sold. In the United States, there are also performance royalties for the digital performance of masters, which includes streaming and satellite radio. Outside of the United States, there are also performance royalties payable for the performance of master recordings on terrestrial radio (known as "neighboring rights"), but that right does not exist in the United States.

In addition, there are master use fees[5], which are not royalties, but negotiated fees paid between the production and the master owner to synchronize a master recording with an audio-visual production, like a film, TV, or other audio-visual production. The master use fee for the master and the synchronization fee for the composition are often set at the same price so they are treated equally, but that has to be specified in the license. Again, a master use fee is not a royalty, but it is an additional income stream for masters.

All Together Now!

Here's an example tying many of the types of uses together to illustrate how one piece of music can be used and generate royalties in the real world. To be clear, when I say a royalty is earned for the publisher or the label, those royalties are usually split with the songwriter or artist based on contract, which will be explained later.

First, an artist writes a musical composition and then records that composition on an album. All sales of physical goods (like CDs) and digital downloads generate mechanical royalties for the composition, as well as streaming mechanicals when the music is streamed on interactive services. The composition also earns performance royalties when the composition is played on the radio, and streamed. The master recording will earn royalties from sales and streaming, as well as digital performance royalties when streamed and played on satellite radio.

Now let's say this piece of music is later used in a film. There is an upfront sync fee for the musical composition, and a master use fee for the master recording in order to use the song in the production (to synchronize the audio with the visual media). The production also would like the song to appear on the film's soundtrack album, so the label releasing the soundtrack pays mechanical royalties to the music publisher for sales (physical and downloads) of that soundtrack (or individual track download), and if streamed, the composition earns a streaming mechanical (paid by the streaming service) and public performance royalty. The record label or master owner will enjoy sales royalties (shared with the artist) as well as reproduction payments and digital performance royalties on the streams. When that film later airs on TV, it also counts as a public performance for the composition, and it generates more performance royalties.

For marketing purposes, the production also wants to create T-shirts with a lyric line from the composition, because the song featured prominently in the film. This generates a print royalty for the publisher for every T-shirt sold.

Also due to the popularity of the song, other artists record their own "cover" versions, owing mechanical royalties to the publisher for their album/download sales for the composition, and the composition would also earn streaming mechanicals and public performance income when these cover versions are streamed and performed.

There also may be performance income for live concert performances of the composition, as well as additional print opportunities for various products.

This is exactly why there are so many possibilities for earning money from music and one reason why this business is so exciting. If one song is big enough, it can be a huge earner and some artists and/or songwriters have been able to live off the income from a single song!

Chapter Summary

- Compositions and master recordings have royalty streams specific to each type of asset and use.
- Each royalty stream is tied to a right of copyright.
- One song (composition and master together) can generate many different royalty streams.

Chapter Four
Royalty Collection Services

Now that you have an understanding of the different types of royalty streams, this chapter will focus on what you need to do to collect them. Whenever music is being used, it is generating royalties, and failure to properly collect means that you are leaving money on the table. Make sure to take care of your business so your business takes care of you. Here's where to start:

Performance Rights Organizations (PROs)

The first type of royalty collection service is performance rights organizations ("PROs" – pronounced "P-R-Os," not pronounced like an abbreviation for professionals). PROs collect the public performance royalties when compositions are performed publicly on the radio, on television, live, streaming, etc. Once again, these royalties are tied to the public performance right of copyright.

There are four performance rights organizations in the United States. They are the American Society of Composers,

Authors and Publishers (ASCAP), Broadcast Music, Inc. (BMI), SESAC (SESAC), and Global Music Rights (GMR). ASCAP and BMI are non-profit organizations open to anyone who wants to join them. SESAC is by invitation only, and GMR is a private company with its own private clients.

Songwriters need to register with a performance rights organization in three ways for complete registration:

1. As a writer,

2. As a publisher, and

3. Register the individual compositions.

PRO Writer Registration

Every songwriter needs to register as a writer with a performance rights organization to get paid the "writer's share" of performance royalties. This royalty stream is paid directly to writers by the performance rights organizations and does not flow through a music publisher. Songwriters can only register with one performance rights organization at a time. For example, if you choose ASCAP, you can't also register with BMI as a writer, or vice versa. If for some reason you do want to change your affiliation, you can usually do so at a later date, but it is subject to the terms of the agreement with the performance rights organization with which you have already affiliated.

Again, note that a PRO will **_always_** pay the writer's share of performance royalties directly to the songwriter. Those payments will not flow through a music publisher.

PRO Publisher Registration

If you're not already signed with a music publisher, then you are actually your own music publisher, and therefore you also want to register with a performance rights organization as a publisher. You will need to register with the same performance rights organization as a publisher that you are already registered with as a writer. For example, if you're registered with ASCAP as a writer, then you're going to join ASCAP as a publisher as well. If you're a BMI writer, then would register with BMI as a publisher.

You cannot be a writer with one PRO and a publisher with another. The exception to this is if you also publish other writers who are affiliated with a different PRO than you are, then you can join the other PRO as publisher of those writers.

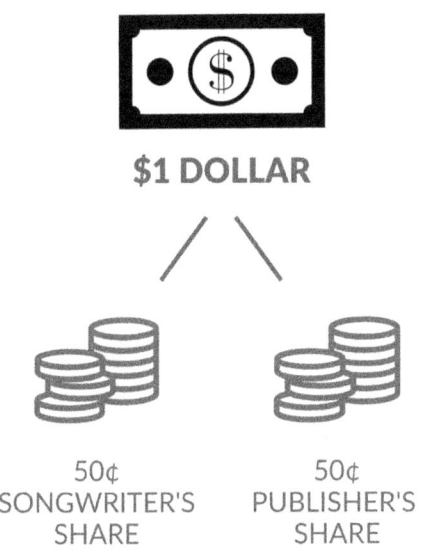

The purpose of registering as a publisher member with a performance rights organization is to collect the "publisher's share" of public performance royalties. The publisher's share is the other half of the income that corresponds to the "writer's share" explained above. When one dollar of performance royalties is earned, half of that is the "writer's share," and the other half of it is the "publisher's share." If you're your own publisher, you want to register as both so that you can collect both halves of that dollar.

Individual Composition Registration

After you are set up as a writer and a publisher, you then need to register the titles, songwriters, publishers, and percentages for all of the individual compositions. The reason for this is that the PRO has to know what compositions to look for when tracking performances, and also who to pay for those compositions.

If you are an ASCAP member, ASCAP divides a composition as follows:

$$100\% \text{ (entire composition)} = \\ 50\% \text{ writer's share} + 50\% \text{ publisher's share}$$

Therefore, if there are two writers on a composition, each with 50%, the ASCAP registration would actually list each writer as having 25%.

In contrast, BMI works on a 200% scale, so

$$200\% \text{ (entire composition)} = \\ 100\% \text{ writer's share} + 100\% \text{ publisher's share}$$

Therefore, if there are two writers on a composition, each with 50%, the BMI registration would list each writer as having 50%.

The publisher's share usually corresponds to the same percentages as their writers, although could vary based on the circumstances.

By registering as a writer and publisher, and registering the individual compositions, the performance rights organization will have the information needed to know what composition to track and who to pay as the writer and publisher of those compositions.

Importance of PRO Registration

Registration with the performance rights organization is important because if you don't register with a performance organization, you won't be paid royalties when your compositions are performed (remember, public performance is more than live concert performances). If you have incorrect registrations, or you're not registered at all, the performance rights organizations will not collect and pay you because they won't know to collect royalties for your composition or that it belongs to you. If for some reason you registered after a composition has already accumulated some performances, the performance rights organizations can only pay previously earned royalties for a limited period of time, which is usually just a few years. Therefore, it is possible that a lot of money could be lost, especially with streaming today. If your music is being performed, you're leaving money on the table by not registering with a performance rights organization.

If you are signed to a publisher, the publisher will be responsible for registering the individual compositions. However, even if your publisher or a member of your team is handling the registrations for you, you should always check to make sure they are correct. I have seen numerous issues where a third party like a team member (and sometimes even a publisher) registers a composition incorrectly and causes the writer to lose money.

Real World Example

In one particular matter I dealt with, a composition was not correctly registered because one of the writers was not registered as a writer with a performance rights organization. This had gone on for decades, and this person probably lost millions of dollars in royalties because it was a famous older song with millions of performances. You don't want that to be you, so make sure you register correctly with a performance rights organization.

To recap, songwriters need to register in three ways with a performance rights organization:

1. As a writer,
2. As a publisher, and
3. Register the individual compositions.

Harry Fox Agency (HFA)

The next royalty collection service that you would want to sign up with is the Harry Fox Agency. Harry Fox collects and pays the mechanical royalties discussed earlier, and it's free to register on their website.

Harry Fox also has an "affiliated publisher" membership for $100, which means Harry Fox can issue mechanical licenses on behalf of that publisher member, and the publisher also has additional benefits like being able to opt into additional license opportunities.

Sound Exchange

The next royalty collection service to register with is SoundExchange. SoundExchange collects royalties for digital performances of master recordings, such as satellite radio and online streaming. It is also free to register with SoundExchange on their website.

YouTube

YouTube Ad Monetization is not a royalty collection service, but it can generate additional revenue, so it's worth mentioning. YouTube Ad Monetization gives video, composition, and master recording owners a percentage of the ad revenue when ads are played on YouTube videos. This feature is not available to everyone, as it requires a certain number of plays and subscribers, but it is something to keep in mind once reaching the eligible level.

Chapter Summary

- Register with a performance rights organization as a writer and a publisher, and register the individual compositions to receive performance royalties.

- Register with the Harry Fox Agency to collect mechanical royalties.

- Register with the other services mentioned in this chapter to collect additional royalty streams.

The Ultimate Royalty Reference Guide

To sum it all up, check out the guide on the next few pages for easy reference for each type of royalty, what right it corresponds to, and who collects and pays those royalties.

The "asset" is the property owned, in this case, the composition or the master recording.

Royalty	Asset	Copyright	Use	Payment Between	Register with
Mechanical	Composition	Reproduction & Distribution	To "mechanically re-produce" and distribute a composition on a master recording.	Paid by record labels to publishers for each record/download manufac-tured/distributed/sold. Music publisher splits with writer based on contract.	Harry Fox Agency If you are signed to a publisher, these payments will come through your publisher.
Streaming Mechanical	Composition	Reproduction & Distribution	Mechanical reproduc-tion of composition data in a stream.	Paid by DSPs[6] to publishers for the data reproduction of a composition during a stream. Music publisher splits with writer based on contract.	Harry Fox Agency If you are signed to a publisher, these payments will come through your publisher.

Royalty	Asset	Copyright	Use	Payment Between	Register with
Synchronization	Composition	Reproduction	Reproduce a composition in timed relation with visual images.	Negotiated contractual fee paid by production to music publisher. Music publisher splits with writer based on contract.	N/A
Performance	Composition	Public performance	When a musical composition is publicly performed on radio, TV, streaming, & live.	Paid from broadcasters/venues/users of music to PROs. PROs then pay music publishers and songwriters. (This includes performance income from streaming.) Music publisher may split with writer based on contract.	ASCAP, BMI, SESAC
Print	Composition	Reproduction	When musical notation or lyrics are reprinted.	Paid from the printer to the music publisher. Music publisher splits with writer based on contract.	N/A

Royalty	Asset	Copyright	Use	Payment Between	Register with
Lyric changes, modifications, medleys, replays, etc.	Composition	Adaptation (Derivative Works)	When someone wants to change a musical composition or use it in a new way (like a sample, replay, or medley). **Must receive prior permission from owner of rights.**	Paid from person/company wanting to make the change to owner of composition. The music publisher and/or songwriter often will own a portion of or the full copyright for the new work. Music publisher splits with writer based on contract.	N/A
Streaming & Satellite Radio	Master	Digital Performance of Master Recordings	Streaming/playing the master recording on streaming services or satellite radio.	Paid by DSPs to SoundExchange for the performance of a master recording during a stream or played on satellite radio. Sound Exchange pays featured artists and labels directly.	Sound Exchange

Royalty	Asset	Copyright	Use	Payment Between	Register with
Sales	Master	Distribution	Sales of physical product / digital downloads.	Paid to master owner/record label, and company splits with artist based on artist's royalty rate.	N/A
Master Use (may also be referred to as synchronization)	Master	Reproduction	Reproduce a master recording in timed relation with visual images.	Negotiated contractual fee paid by production to master owner/record label. Record label splits with artist based on contract.	N/A
Sampling or other modifications	Master	Adaptation (Derivative Works)	When someone wants to use/change a master recording or use a portion of an already existing master recording in a new recording. **Must receive prior permission from owner of rights.**	Paid from person/company wanting to make the change to or use a portion of a master recording. The label splits with artist based on contract.	N/A

Chapter Five
Keep Your Catalogue Clean

Something often overlooked in music resources (actually, I've not seen it discussed in any other books I've read) is keeping the data associated with a music catalogue correct and organized. I've dealt with countless catalogues with really messy information – missing documents, incorrect registrations, works not registered for copyright, etc. Not only is this problematic for new catalogues, but the problems get worse as a catalogue ages because it becomes harder to find the missing puzzle pieces.

The data associated with catalogues is almost as important as the catalogues themselves, so it is a good business practice to keep catalogue information clean. Having correct, organized, and up-to-date information:

- allows for correct payment information,
- facilitates faster and easier licensing for compositions and masters,
- makes a catalogue more desirable for selling at a later date, and

- makes it easier when a catalogue passes to beneficiaries or heirs.

If the data is wrong, collection societies and other companies will often withhold payment until the data is corrected, and potential licensees will not use the song if that is an option. Therefore, your takeaway from this section should be:

Bad Data = No Payment

Chain of Title

"Chain of Title" refers to the copyright ownership of a catalogue over time. An example could be a songwriter originally owned a composition, assigned it to a publisher, then that publisher sold the catalogue to another company and that last company is now the current copyright owner. It is also possible that copyrights may stay with only one owner. Regardless of the details, it is important that this is documented. As already explained, all works should be registered with the Copyright Office. If that ownership changes hands, that change should be recorded with the Copyright Office. This is similar to purchasing a house: the previous owner "had title to" (owned) the house, and then when you purchase the house, the deed of transfer is recorded with the county, and then it is *on record* that you are the current owner of the house.

Keep a record of all titles, copyright registration (or recordation) dates, and copyright registration (or recordation) numbers.

Author and Third Party Information

In addition to keeping track of the chain of title information described above, it is also beneficial to keep a record of any co-writer or co-owner and publisher names, contact information, ownership and royalty participation percentages, label information, as well as any associated identification numbers.

Some of these identification numbers include:

- **IPI:** This is an identification number given by a performance rights organization to songwriters and music publishers and helps to identify each party for payment and registrations.

- **Work ID:** This is an identification number given by a performance rights organization to each individual composition registered.

- **HFA Song Code:** This is an identification number given by the Harry Fox Agency to identify each composition registered with HFA.

- **ISWC:** International Standard Work Code is an international identification number given to compositions. This is used to identify the composition, but also match it with the master recordings on which it appears.

- **ISRC:** International Standard Recording Code is an international identification number given to master recordings. This is used to identify the master recording, but also match it with the compositions recorded on the master recordings.

There are more codes, but these are the basic ones to get started.

Keeping clear records of all of the ownership or income shares, along with the information correctly identifying the compositions and masters, will make it faster and easier to provide this information to licensees and royalty collection services. This makes it easier for you to get business done and receive payments because you don't have to hunt around for the information every time or tell a business partner you don't know the information. It also makes it easier for those working with you to use your music, and in this business, music that is easy to work with gets used more often.

You don't need any fancy software, procedures, or staff to do this. You can keep this information on a simple spreadsheet.

Chapter Summary

- Keep organized records of copyright ownership information, as well as co-writer and other ownership and identification information.
- This can be easily done on a spreadsheet; you don't need fancy software. See Appendix A for resources.
- Keeping a clean catalogue helps you do business and get paid more efficiently, and makes your music easy with which to work.
- Remember, bad data = no payment.

PART III
Music Agreements

Chapter Six
Contract Terms

There are certain contract terms that regularly confuse non-lawyers, so here's a brief glossary of some common contract terms that confuse people.

Usually terms that end in "-or" such as Assignor, Grantor, Licensor, etc. is the person or company giving the rights, and terms that end in "-ee" like Assignee, Grantee, and Licensee are those receiving the rights.

Advance: This is a payment of royalties in advance. The company must recoup (earn back) this money before they pay you royalties (see "Recoupable" definition below). Let me be very clear, an advance is a LOAN. See more in Chapter Eight about how advances work.

Assign/Assignment: This term is usually used in relation to copyright and means one party is transferring ownership of a copyright or copyrights to another party.

Buy-out: This means that another party is buying out all of your ownership rights (or you are buying theirs), including the right to receive income. It may be that there are certain income streams that you are still allowed to receive, but it depends on the agreement.

Exclusive: In regard to an exclusive term deal or exclusive representation deal, this means that the company who has the exclusive rights to your services and/or music is the only one allowed to promote and benefit from them. For example, if you are under an exclusive agreement with a record label, you can't sign with another label until the term of the contract with the label has ended. Similarly, if a song is subject to an exclusive agreement, rights to that song cannot be granted to another party.

Exclusive License: An exclusive license means that the Licensee is the only one that gets to use the rights and the Licensor cannot grant those rights to anyone else as per the terms of the agreement.

Non-Exclusive License: A non-exclusive license means that the Licensee is *not* the only one that gets to use the rights and the Licensor *can* grant those rights to others.

Perpetuity: Forever.

Recoupable: Recoupable means that a company who gave you an advance has the right to recoup, i.e. earn back, the amount of money they advanced you before they pay you any royalties.

Royalties: Income paid for the use of your music. Depending on the royalty in question (refer back to Chapter 3), this may be paid directly to you from a collection society, or from a company.

Term: How long something lasts, such as a contract or license.

Territory: The geographical locations governed by the agreement. It may be certain countries, the world, or the universe.

Work for Hire / Work Made for Hire: The employer or hiring party is the owner of the work and considered the legal author of the work for copyright purposes.

Chapter Seven
Music Publishing Agreements

All music starts with a composition, which is one of the reasons why I love the area of music publishing.

Music Publishing is the management of the compositions (what is called "administration" in the industry) and involves issuing and otherwise handling licenses, collecting royalties, making sure uses of the compositions are correctly paid, etc. "Publishing royalties" is an umbrella term for all composition royalties. Publishing royalties are split into what is known as the "publisher's share" and the "writer's share." Traditionally, the publisher's share and writer's share are split 50/50. This is how royalty collection societies will divide it, but how much the writer receives may vary by contract with the publisher, whereby the publisher may take a lesser percentage and pay more to the writer.

The percentage arrangements can vary based on the type of agreement with the music publisher, so here is a quick overview of the most typical structures of music publishing agreements.

PUBLISHING ROYALTIES

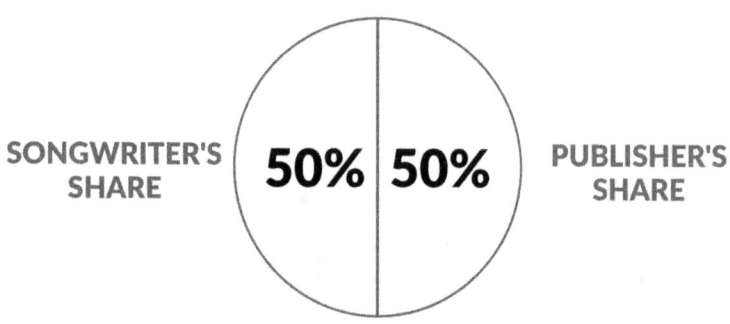

Songwriter Agreement

A songwriter agreement usually involves a writer transferring 100% of the copyright ownership in a writer's compositions (it could be a single composition, all compositions in a catalogue and/or all compositions written during the term of the agreement) to a music publisher and a 50/50 income split between the publisher and the writer. While the writer will be under contract with the publisher for a certain term (i.e. number of years), the transfer of copyright to the publisher will last for the full length of the copyright term.[7] This is consistent with the splits described above whereby the writer keeps the writer's share and the publisher keeps the publisher's share. While these were some of the most common agreements 60 years ago and are still used today, they aren't entered into as often because many writers value owning their content more in today's music market. This model (with some modifications) is also used frequently in music library agreements.

COMPOSITION COPYRIGHT OWNERSHIP

PUBLISHING ROYALTIES

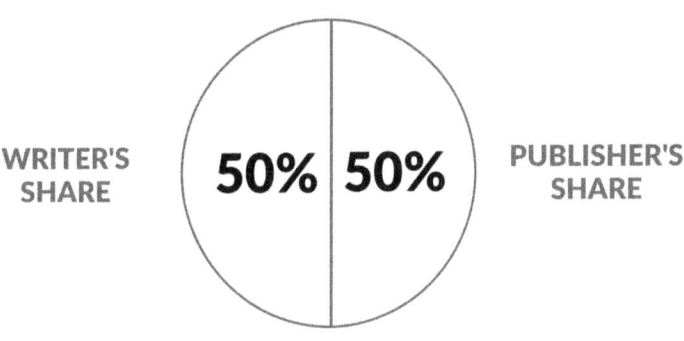

Songwriter Agreement Examples

Co-Publishing Agreement

A Co-Publishing Agreement is very common today and involves a writer transferring 50% of the copyright ownership of the compositions in the catalogue to the music publisher and an income split of 75/25 where 75% goes to the writer and 25% goes to the publisher. Basically, the writer gets the full 50% writer's share, and the publisher pays half of the publisher's share to the writer and keeps the other half of the publisher's share for itself. Keep in mind that like a Songwriter Agreement, the writer will be under contract with the publisher for a certain term (i.e. number of years), and the transfer of 50% of the copyright to the publisher will last for the full length of the copyright term.[8]

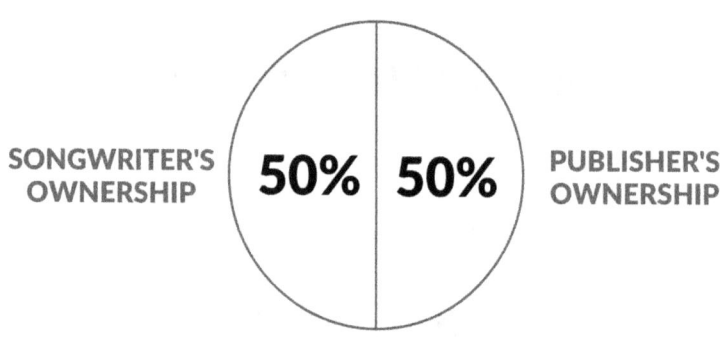

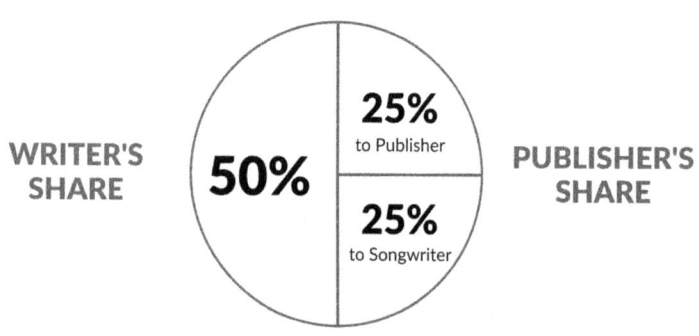

Co-Publishing Agreement Examples

54 | Don't Get Screwed

Administration Agreement

An Administration Agreement is also very popular today and involves no copyright transfer — the publisher administers without owning copyright. Administration agreements are most available to established songwriters, but may also be offered to independent writers still growing their careers and catalogues. The royalty splits on these agreements vary, but generally the administrator will take a fee of 10-25% for doing the administration (although there are some outliers and circumstances that might vary that percentage).

COMPOSITION COPYRIGHT OWNERSHIP

PUBLISHING ROYALTIES

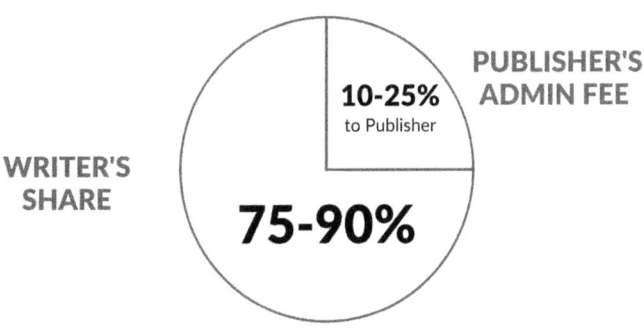

Administration Agreement Examples

A Note About Splits

Writers talk a lot about "splits," but this term can refer to more than one concept depending on the context. "Splits" refers to the division of royalties between more than one party. For example, the 50/50 royalty split in a Songwriter Agreement and 75/25 royalty split in a Co-Publishing Agreement discussed above are "splits" between the songwriter and publisher. However, when multiple songwriters co-write a composition together, those are also known as "splits" because the royalties will be split based on the percentage of the composition attributed to a specific songwriter. Because a music publisher only has the authority to publish and collect income for its songwriter's share, the amount that a writer and publisher will split will be based on the writer's share (or split) of a particular composition.

Another important fact is that splits must **_always_** add up to 100%. More than 100% percent of any entity or asset does not exist in reality, and a figure of less than 100% means that there is a share not accounted for. If your splits add up to more or less than 100%, go back and do them again.

Note that "splits" do not necessarily refer to copyright. While co-writers would, in principle, each have percentage of ownership of the copyright to the composition, that is not something that is listed on the copyright registration certificate. Copyright law provides that joint ownership in a copyright is held in a structure called joint tenancy. This makes the most sense when comparing ownership of a copyright to ownership of a piece of property, like a house. When two people own a house together (such as a married couple), they both own the entire house together; the house isn't divided with an imaginary line down the center or ownership of certain rooms allocated to each person. Similarly, both owners will own the entire copyright, but will only be able to transact and collect on their percentage share as designated by contract. This is why, as will be explained in the section on Songwriter Split Agreements in Chapter 9, massive problems ensue when it is not clear what percentage of a composition is attributable to each writer.

Here are some examples of how it would work:

Let's say two songwriters co-write a composition and "split" the composition 50/50 (see Example 1 on the next page). Writer 1 has a Co-Publishing Agreement with a music publisher, and Writer 2 has an Administration Agreement with a different publisher, with such publisher taking a 25% administration fee.

To show a different configuration, let's say two songwriters co-write a composition and "split" the composition 50/50 (see Example 2 on the following page). Writer 1 has a Songwriter Agreement with a music publisher, and Writer 2 has a Co-Publishing Agreement with a different publisher.

Today, it is very common for compositions to have anywhere between three to nine writers on a composition (sometimes more!), so you can imagine how complicated determining splits and income collection can get. This problem is further exacerbated by third parties (like producers) wanting songwriter credit without composing the composition, which I discuss more in the section on Producer Agreements in Chapter 9.

Example 1

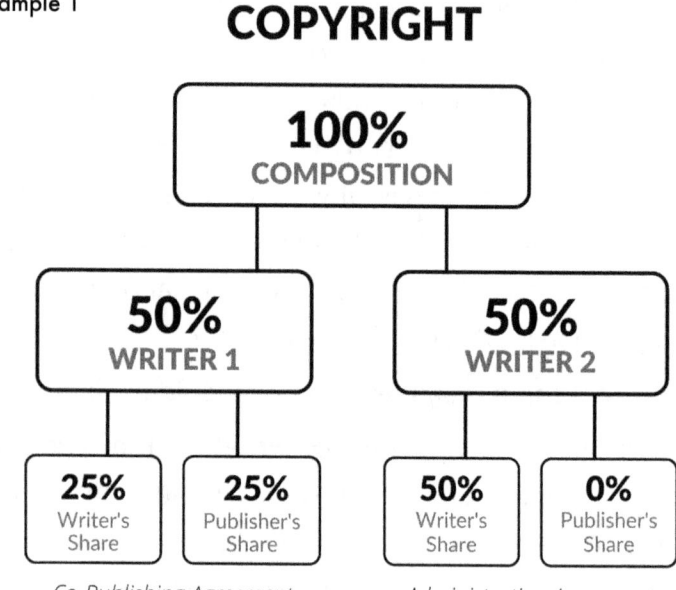

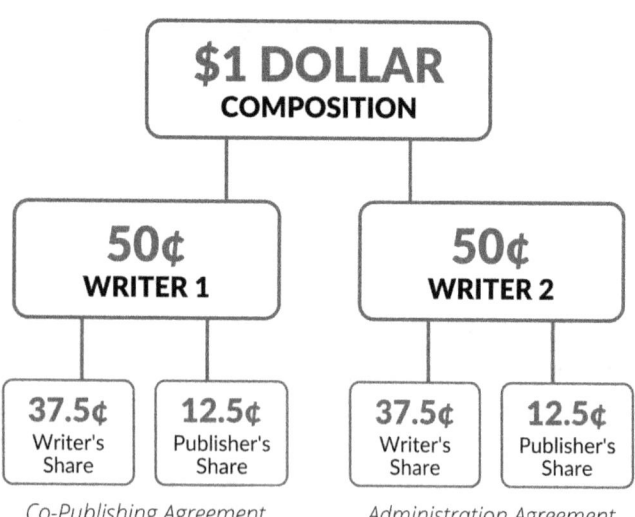

Example 2

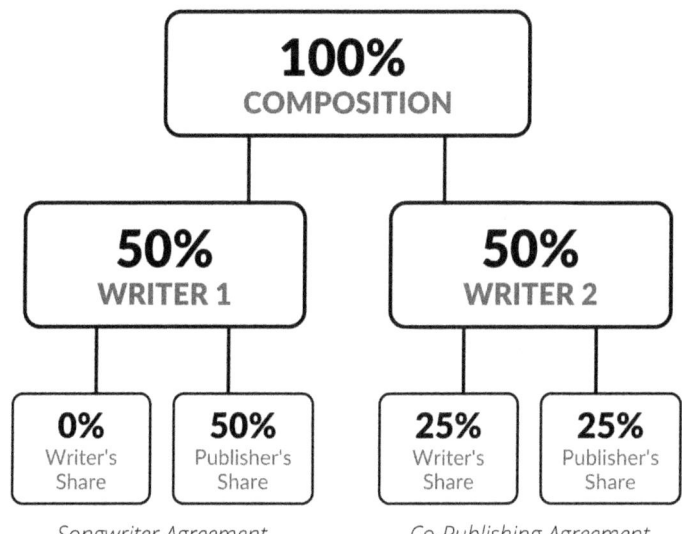

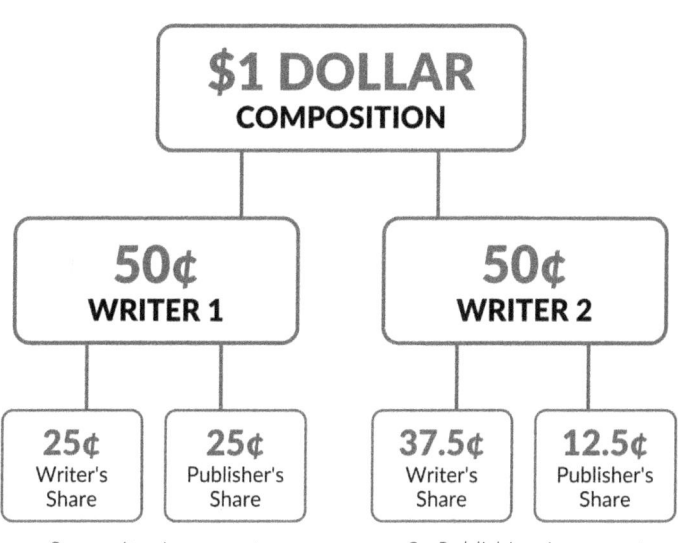

Other General Terms

Publishing agreements, like other contracts, will also have some other aspects discussed like term, territory, exclusivity, etc. A basic way to understand publishing agreements is that the writer is under contract for the publisher to represent the writer's compositions for a period of time (term), which the publisher may or may not own, and in exchange, the publisher will exploit that music, collect the royalties, and split those royalties with the writer. However, these agreements and the terms they contain can get complicated, so it is always best to have a publishing agreement reviewed by an experienced music attorney to make sure the agreement is fair and that you understand what you are signing.

Chapter Summary

- The writer's share and the publisher's share of income is traditionally split 50/50, but that can vary by contract.
- Composition ownership can vary by contract.
- It is always best to have a publishing agreement reviewed before signing.

Chapter Eight
Recording Agreements

Recording agreements or "record deals" have traditionally been seen as the ultimate way to "make it" in the music business. The internet has changed the landscape of how music is discovered, making exposure more accessible to an independent musician. However, there are many artists still interested in signing with a label. The complexities of recording agreements have filled entire books, but this chapter will focus on a few practical points to get you started in understanding how recording agreements work.

Traditional Recording Agreements

A very basic explanation of the traditional structure of recording agreements is that an artist records exclusively for one company during the term of the agreement, the label owns the recordings the artist makes during that term, the label pays the money upfront for recording costs, marketing expenses, etc., gets the records into the marketplace for sale, and then does a lot of promotion to try to make it sell millions of copies. Once the label recoups its initial financial investment, the label splits any profits with the artist according to the artist's royalty rate.

However, recording agreements have always been more complicated than their surface appearance. The way royalties are calculated are often based on different models and include various deductions that ultimately reduce the amount available to split with the artist. Labels are also potentially involved with touring, music videos, websites, and other assets that go along with an artist's career, and therefore each of those aspects have their own practices in the agreements.

There are other books[9] that go through detailed examples and calculations of each of these aspects, but a real-world, big picture understanding is what I am trying to convey here. The biggest aspect of recording agreements (and really any music agreements) that artists don't understand, is that an advance is a loan. Anytime a label puts up money for recording costs, living expenses, marketing costs, producer royalties, composition royalties, tour expenses, video costs, etc., it is treated as an advance. This means that the label fronts the money, and then recoups it from the sales/streaming/etc. income generated from your recordings, and the label must make back its investment before ever sharing the profits with you in the form of your royalty.

There is a great scene in the movie *Cadillac Records*, where the Muddy Waters character asks the Leonard Chess character (the owner of Chess Records) if royalties had come in from one of his songs, as he needed funds. The Leonard Chess character told Muddy he already gave him his royalties, which confused Muddy. Chess pointed to the Cadillac that Muddy was driving, previously given to him by Chess, and said, "The Cadillac ain't free, Mud," meaning that the cost of the Cadillac was treated as an advance that needed to be recouped from record sales revenue. The Muddy character had originally thought the Cadillac was a gift, and finally understood that these "perks" were actually loans against his royalty income.

360 Deals

After the music industry was hit hard by the illegal downloading era, record labels started a practice of signing artists to "360 Deals." The name refers to the 360 degrees of a circle, because the label was seeking to share in all rights of an artist's career – recording, publishing, merchandising, touring, endorsements, etc. For a time, major labels would not even sign new artists unless they signed 360 deals. There were also variations of these deals we called 180 deals, 270 deals, etc., which means they encompassed multiple career areas, but not all of them.

360 Deals came in two forms, which I call, "Ownership of Rights Deals" and "Income Participation Deals."[10] Ownership of Rights Deals described when labels owned these additional rights and actively exploited them, such as the label owning any musical compositions written by an artist and acting as the music publisher. Income Participation Deals described when the label did not own or actively exploit any of these additional rights, but the artist agreed via contract to share income from those other areas with the label.

Both of these agreements were largely unfair and problematic, but got the labels through a tough time when income was down and before streaming became commonplace. Currently, 360 Deals are still in practice, but have become less common, with more deals focusing either on solely recording, or recording plus one or two other rights, such as publishing.

Word of Caution

Although it is beyond the intention of this book to go through all the nuances of recording agreements, I cannot stress enough the fact that these deals get extremely complicated and have incredibly complex terms that require an attorney's skill to decipher. If you are seeking or offered a recording agreement, do not proceed without the advice and representation of an experienced music attorney.

Chapter Summary

- An advance is a loan and the label has to recoup that loan before paying an artist royalties.
- Any payments for the artist are usually advances, so know what is an advance and what is not.
- Always get a recording agreement reviewed before signing.

Chapter Nine
Agreements Needed for Independent Musicians

There are a few types of agreements that are the most essential for independent musicians, and even those who are signed with a publisher or record company. Below I explain the most needed agreements for independent musicians, why they are needed, how to get them, and the bad things that can happen without them.

Songwriter Split Agreements

When co-writing with others, it is imperative to have what is called a "Songwriter Split Agreement." This is a short agreement that lists the writers of the compositions, ownership and royalty percentages of the composition, and whether the writers are administering their own shares of the composition or whether somebody else is doing so on their behalf. There are longer versions of this Songwriter Split Agreement, but this is the minimum required.

A Songwriter Split Agreement can offer proof if there is a dispute later about who wrote the composition, or if someone that wasn't credited on the song says he or she should be credited as a writer or receive royalties.

I am often asked what percentages should be assigned to each writer. The traditional method is that two writers are 50/50, three writers are 1/3 each, and four writers are a quarter each. While this method is still used by some writers, the percentage perspective has evolved to be based more on what each writer has contributed and assigning a percentage comparable to that contribution. While compositions have traditionally been written by one to three, and sometimes four people, there are now sometimes eight or nine writers on a single composition! My personal philosophy has been to assign percentages based on contribution, but you have to decide what works best for you and your co-writers, and that may differ depending on the composition and with whom you are writing.

Real World Example

Several years ago, there was a new band that had written some songs in the studio while recording their first record. As is very typical, the band had some friends and girlfriends in the studio with them. One of the songs written during these recording sessions became a big hit and was making a lot of money. However, the band did not complete a Songwriter Split Agreement while they were writing these songs in the studio. After the song became a hit, one of the band member's girlfriends, who had become an ex-girlfriend, called the band and told them they promised her ten percent of the composition royalties for writing a certain line. The band denied promising a percentage to her, so she hired a lawyer. While this woman did not necessarily have proof that she wrote this particular line in the song or that she was owed ten percent, the band did not have any proof that she did not write that line of the song or that she was not owed the ten percent. The solution involved a choice of either going to court (which could have resulted in a win for either side since neither of them had any proof to support their positions) or settling with this woman and giving her the ten percent of the income for the song. The band chose to give her the ten percent because it was cheaper and easier than fighting the matter in court, spending a few hundred thousand dollars doing so, and potentially losing. Thus, the moral of this story is that they should have had a Songwriter Split Agreement, because that agreement would have served as proof of who was entitled to shares of the song, and the amount of those shares.

This is one of many examples in which writers cannot agree on splits or there is some other type of split dispute, which I also referred to in Chapter 7. Split disputes can result in situations where the song cannot be released, or if it is released, companies and collection societies will put the royalties on hold. This actually happens more than you would think with both independent and famous writers, and it is not a situation you want to be in.

People often ask me when to have a Songwriter Split Agreement signed. They feel awkward presenting the agreement while in the studio because it kills the creative vibe, but the best time to complete a Songwriter Split Agreement is at the time the song is created because it is fresh in everyone's minds.

Signing a Songwriter Split Agreement at the time of creation benefits everyone, so co-writers should appreciate the fact that everybody will be protected when signing this agreement rather than just trying to appear cool by pretending the business side doesn't matter. That attitude is precisely what has "screwed" many musicians. This is your business and protecting it is cool!

Another situation where a Songwriter Split Agreement is important, is to prevent a producer or other hired third party from claiming a larger share of a song than the percentage to which that person is entitled. Not only is the Songwriter Split Agreement important if your producer is a songwriter, but this also comes into play with producer agreements.

Producer Agreements

Musicians often come to me when they're having problems with their producer. Many times, it's because the producer is not turning over the masters, or other times one party feels that the other party is claiming more of an ownership or income percentage than earned. The source of these problems is usually because there was no agreement in writing, and the parties each had their own interpretation of the situation.

These misunderstandings create a lot of problems that can delay or prevent releases of the music and can easily be avoided by having a written producer agreement signed upfront. Producer agreements provide the terms for an unrelated related third party brought in to help in the creation and crafting of the sound of a particular set of music. Always remember that a producer is not the same as another band member or a writer. A good producer agreement will clarify ownership, royalty splits, advances or fees, number of masters being recorded, how and when they can be re-recorded, etc. Sometimes producers do have claims to master ownership and they usually do get upfront fees and a percentage of royalties, but those amounts are negotiated. The ranges tend to vary based on genre and status of the artist and of the producer, as well as other factors.

I'm also often asked whether a producer should receive songwriter credit and/or a percentage of publishing. The answer to this again varies based on the situation. There are certain situations where working with a particular producer will be greatly beneficial to an artist's career and the artist must give up something like a percentage of songwriter credit/ownership in order to work with that producer. Other times, the producer has actually contributed to writing some of the compositions appearing on the album. Lastly, there are times where the producer actually didn't write any portion of the composition but tries to get a piece of the publishing in order to make up for the fact that (s)he won't make much money just from the producer's fee and royalties. Again, I'm a proponent of people getting a percentage on what they contribute, but the decision here really depends on a variety of factors.

Real World Example

Several years ago a band hired me for a consultation, and when I spoke with the band, they explained that the band had hired a producer for their new album and this producer was also in charge of hiring other producers to participate on the project.

During the recording process, the band fired all the producers except the original one due to creative differences. The original producer then hired an entirely new set of producers. Naturally, the first wave of producers expected compensation for the work they had already done and were promised percentages, and the second set of producers were also promised percentages. When the album was finally completed, the band was left with a total of about *ten* percent ownership on both the compositions and masters. Nothing was in writing, but the band was now in a situation that would be hard to prove, and the band didn't have the money to litigate (i.e. sue / fight in court).

I asked the band why they didn't say anything or get a written agreement to protect their rights and the band said, "well, we just sort-of hoped it would get better." As a result of their inaction, the band was in a position where they had to accept this situation as it was, because otherwise their choices were not releasing the album after already paying five figures in costs, or litigation, which was financially not an option.

I felt so bad for them because they were screwed, as trying to change the terms would have resulted in disputes with all of the producers, ultimately blocking the release of the album and any earnings from it.

Real World Example

Another example showing the importance of having a producer agreement negotiated upfront, happened when a client of mine called me to tell me the band was recording a new album and needed me to negotiate the producer agreement. They sent me the producer agreement and the terms were so unfair that the royalty was about five times what it should have been. I called the band and explained the ridiculous terms and asked if they still wanted to work with this producer. They explained to me the album was already completed. Because the album was finished, the producer had minimal incentive to negotiate. It worked out fine in the end because I negotiated it, but other situations might not have had the same result.

Negotiating early in this case is important because the band could have been in a situation where they would not have been able to release their album, they would have had to re-record their album with another producer (costing more money), or they would have had to just give the producer what the producer wanted. Don't be in that situation. Have a proper agreement in place from the beginning so everybody knows what to expect. That way everybody will be happy with the terms, and everybody can work together effectively so that the album can be released.

Band Agreements

A band agreement is vital in helping independent musicians that perform in a band from getting screwed. Every band is different. All the members can be songwriters, some of the members can be songwriters, and occasionally, songwriters may be from outside the band. In some bands, only the main members may share royalties, and the other band members are just considered to be employees who are paid a salary or paid per gig. In other bands, all the income from the band and the expenses are split and may or may not be split equally. There are many different factors affecting bands that need to be laid out in writing, because it can get confusing and contentious when people don't agree on these matters.

Another matter that often arises for bands, is the ownership and or use of the band's name. Often the matters that come up for bands regarding the band's name are who owns and can use the band name, what happens when certain band members leave the band, and if they do leave the band, how those members can use the band name, if at all. There are also other factors of ownership like ownership of the compositions, masters, equipment, etc.

It may vary by state, but in California where I'm licensed, when band members are in a band and there's no written agreement, they are considered to be a general partnership, which means they share all the profits equally, but also have to split all the liabilities equally. That means if somebody makes a mistake and costs the band a lot of money, everybody in the band is liable for those costs equally.

You don't want to be in a situation where either you're not getting your fair share of a band, or you're personally liable for other band members, so it's best to have a written band agreement in place.

The time to put a band agreement in place is in the beginning when you start working with these people and form the band, because when a band is formed, everybody is on good terms and excited to be working together. When the band is breaking up, everybody hates each other, and it's more difficult to come to a resolution. Some bands never come to an agreement and the music and royalties are on hold indefinitely, which means no one gets paid if the music is already released, and if not, the music cannot be released or used at all.

If you are starting a band and bring up topics of a band agreement, ownership, royalties, etc., and one or more people in this band start becoming really difficult, that might be a warning sign not to be in a band with this person or these people. If they are going to be that difficult in the beginning, they are probably going to be more difficult at the end when people aren't on good terms.

Again, this is for everyone's protection and it really gives you a sense of what these people are like. Being in a band with people is almost like being in a marriage, and you want to know what you're getting into before the divorce.

Real World Example

One day I got a call from a musician who was in a band that has been together for about two or three years but was now breaking up. This band did not have a band agreement and had not discussed how the ownership or the royalties were to be split or who could use the band name.

This guy was potentially at risk of losing everything that he had put into this band over the last two or three years. He was potentially losing the right to profit from or even own the results of all his hard work, all his writing, and all his performances. Had the band created a written band agreement at the beginning, they could have laid out what happened in the event of a band break up, from who owns what, to how everything would get split. Even though the members didn't get along anymore, they would have at least had a plan as far as how to move forward and to what everyone was entitled.

Work for Hire Agreements

Another important agreement in certain situations for independent musicians is a Work Made For Hire Agreement. This agreement is basically stating the person who is the employer or hiring party will be the person that's going to be the owner of the work that is the subject of the agreement. Composers, songwriters, and session musicians are regularly asked to sign work for hire agreements. Both those hiring and being hired ask me whether they need a work for hire agreement or whether they should sign one.

Many of these deals will still provide for writer's share of income, or credit, or royalty split, but some may be on a flat fee or buyout basis. It's best to consult with an experienced music attorney to see if you need a work for hire agreement or if you should sign one. In certain circumstances it might be fine, or in other circumstances you might be signing away ownership or royalties that you should not. On the other side, you should know if you need to have people sign work for hire agreements and what the terms should be.

A very important point to note that is often misunderstood in the music industry is that paying for something does **not** mean that you own it. Transfers of copyright ownership are by written agreement only with express language to make the transfer, and work made for hire agreements require additional specific language to be effective. The most common instance this confuses people is when a band hires a photographer to take photographs. The band members think they own the photographs because they paid the photographer for the service. However, unless there is a written agreement where the language specifically states that the photographer transfers copyright ownership to the band, the photographer continues to own the copyrights in those photographs and the band only has a license to use those photographs for purposes like album art, promotional uses, etc. The same principle can apply to session musicians, producers, recording studios, and others, despite custom and practice in the industry. Even if you paid someone to play or sing on your recording, you still need an agreement in place to own the rights to that person's performance. That is why I always make sure my clients have the proper agreements with the proper language in place to ensure they own what they need, and to protect them from others trying to claim ownership later.

Getting the Agreements You Need

One way to get the agreements discussed is to have an experienced music attorney draft them for you. I draft all the agreements discussed in my practice on a daily basis. The advantage of having an agreement drafted for you is that it will be tailored to your needs and the details of your situation, and your attorney can structure the agreement in a manner to serve your best interests.

The other option is to get high-quality contract templates from a website like Indie Artist Resource. I have drafted the templates on Indie Artist Resource based on contracts that I use in my own practice, so I know that they cover the majority of terms that need to be covered in the various agreements. Remember to keep in mind that templates are a great solution for those on a budget, but are only customizable to someone's specific situation where the template allows.

Take caution with other free (and sometimes paid) templates you will find online because not all templates are created equal. I've seen a lot of templates online that are really awful, and I've seen many people trying to use templates that don't fit their situation or that have terms not in their favor.

When to Hire an Attorney

It is always advisable to have an experienced music attorney review agreements, especially if you don't understand them. Even if you do feel that you understand them, it's still a good idea to have them reviewed. I have seen many situations where an artist or writer has read over an agreement that is very similar to other agreements that they have signed previously, and they think they understand all the terms. However, sometimes there's been sneaky legal language in these agreements that I was able to spot as a trained attorney, but that wouldn't be apparent to someone who is not an attorney working with these contracts every day.

If you are not yet at a position in your career where you have contracts to draft or review, you can also set up consultation calls with an attorney to go over questions. I have many clients that will schedule periodic calls with me to discuss questions in regard to their careers or copyrights.

In addition, people on the other side tend to pay more attention to you when an attorney represents you. It elevates your status in their eyes, shows you are professional that takes your business seriously, and they know they can't try to fool you because your attorney will see through it.

It is true fees for attorneys can be expensive. However, it's always recommended to consult with a licensed attorney who is experienced in the type of work that you need, in this case, music agreements and copyright. This is an important investment in your career. I say this not as an advertisement, but because it will benefit you to make sure your career matters are handled properly, your songs are registered correctly, etc. Thinking that you'll save the money by not paying the fees upfront will usually mean that you'll pay higher fees later, because it takes a lot more time and effort to try to fix a messy catalogue or to fix a dispute than negotiate a fair deal in the beginning. Again, if a person is really not in a position to pay attorney fees for custom drafted agreements, then use Indie Artist Resource.

Chapter Summary

- Important agreements for independent artists include a Songwriter Split Agreement, Producer Agreement, Band Agreement, and Work for Hire Agreement.
- Have an attorney draft these agreements for you or get templates from Indie Artist Resource.
- See Appendix A for where to download the templates mentioned in this book.
- Always seek the advice of an experienced attorney when dealing with contracts.

Conclusion

Now you know about why copyright registration is essential and what it means to actually own a copyright, the different types of royalties and how they apply in the real world, how to get paid the royalties your music earns, the contracts most needed by independent musicians, and how you can avoid mistakes made by musicians in the past.

As I said in the beginning, it is possible to protect yourself and your career with the right knowledge and action along with guidance from the right representatives. Remember that this is your business and you need to look after it.

I wish you the best of luck, and please contact me at www.themusicindustrylawyer.com if I can be of assistance in your music career.

Notes

1. Results not guaranteed.
2. For The Beatles' trivia buffs and those that care to know, "Yesterday" was actually written solely by Sir Paul McCartney, but credited as Lennon/McCartney because Lennon and McCartney had an agreement that any composition written by either of them for The Beatles would be credited as such. McCartney later tried to get Yoko Ono (Lennon's widow) to agree to change the credit to McCartney's name only, but she refused.
3. 17 U.S. Code §102(a).
4. 17 U.S. Code §302(a). Any works created after January 1, 1978 will have a term of life of the author plus 70 years. However, older works have a different term. For works created prior to January 1, 1978, there was an initial term of 28 years, plus a renewal term of 28 years which later was extended to 67 years, giving pre-1978 works a total term of 95 years. Note there are a lot of exceptions and nuances that can affect these older term lengths (such as whether the work needed to be renewed) so

it is best to consult with an attorney with expertise in copyright law to know the exact term of protection for the work.

5. Master Use fees are often referred to also as synchronization fees even though that term technically is only attributable to the synchronization of musical compositions.

6. DSPs are "digital service providers," most notably Google, Amazon, Spotify, Pandora, and Apple.

7. Unless the contract has language that allows for a reversion of rights after a certain period of time or when certain circumstances occur. There are also provisions in the U.S. Copyright Law that will allow for a statutory reversion right if the proper notices are filed at the designated times.

8. Unless the contract has language that allows for a reversion of rights after a certain period of time or when certain circumstances occur. There are also provisions in the U.S. Copyright Law that will allow for a statutory reversion right if the proper notices are filed at the designated times.

9. A great, more detailed book to start with to learn more about record deals and royalties is *All You Need to Know About the Music Business* by Donald Passman. For a more indepth look at publishing, there is *Music, Money, and Success* by Jeff Brabec and Todd Brabec, and *Music Publishing – The Complete Guide* by Steve Winogradsky.

10. For more information regarding "Ownership of Rights Deals" v. "Income Participation Deals", check out my

article, "360 Deals and the California Talent Agencies Act: Are Record Labels Procuring Employment?", published in *Entertainment and Sports Lawyer*, a publication of the ABA Forum on the Entertainment and Sports Industries, Vol. 29, No. 3, Fall 2011.

Appendix A

Templates and Resources

The templates and other resources mentioned in this book are available for download at www.indieartistresource.com.

Websites and Organizations

United States Copyright Office – www.copyright.gov

United States Patent and Trademark Office – www.uspto.gov

American Society of Composers, Authors and Publishers (ASCAP) – www.ascap.com

Broadcast Music, Inc. (BMI) – www.bmi.com

SESAC (SESAC) – www.sesac.com

Global Music Rights (GMR) – www.globalmusicrights.com

Harry Fox Agency – www.harryfox.com

SoundExchange – www.soundexchange.com

YouTube – www.youtube.com

Acknowledgments

Writing this book has been an exciting experience and one I am glad to share with you.

I've had a variety of teachers, mentors, and colleagues who have contributed to my understanding of this fantastic industry over many years of schooling and legal practice. You all know who you are, and I thank you for your individual contributions.

Thank you to my clients who trust me to protect them, whereby we deal with these concepts on a daily basis.

Thank you to those of you who continually read my articles and attend my speaking events. You showed me the need for this book in the industry.

Thank you to my assistant, Karlee Hormell, for all her work on graphics and assisting with plans and preparation for the book's release and tour; and thank you to interns, Conner Couch, Aaron Black, Reanne Helo, and Lance Pierre for their assistance and feedback in the book's initial stages.

Most importantly, thank you to my fantastic parents for their enduring love and support. Your guidance has helped me to be the best that I can be, and I am forever grateful.

About the Author

Erin M. Jacobson is a practicing attorney, experienced deal negotiator, and a seasoned advisor of intellectual property rights who protects musicians, songwriters, music publishers, and a wide variety of other music professionals.

Ms. Jacobson's clients include Grammy and Emmy Award winners, legacy artists and catalogues, heirs and estates, and independent artists and companies. Ms. Jacobson regularly handles all types of agreements within the music industry, with an emphasis on music publishing, licensing, and catalogue acquisitions. In addition, she is one of the leading attorneys on copyright recapture and termination issues.

Ms. Jacobson also places special emphasis on her work with legacy clients and their catalogues, as her knowledge of both classic music and current industry practices places her in a unique position to protect and revitalize older catalogues.

Ms. Jacobson has been named as one of the "Top Music Lawyers" by *Billboard*, as well as a Super Lawyers Rising Star and one of the Top Women Attorneys in Southern California. In addition, Ms. Jacobson is a frequent author and speaker, and has been featured in publications including *Billboard* and *Forbes*. She also serves on the Board of Directors for the Association of Independent Music Publishers (AIMP).

Ms. Jacobson is the author of the book, *Don't Get Screwed! How to Protect Yourself as an Independent Musician*. She also founded and owns Indie Artist Resource, the independent musician's resource for legal and business protection. Indie Artist Resource offers templates for agreements most needed by independent musicians, as well as a variety of educational materials to empower independent musicians to make informed decisions about their careers.

More information on Ms. Jacobson and her law practice in Beverly Hills, CA can be found at:

www.themusicindustrylawyer.com.

Indie Artist Resource can be found at:

www.indieartistresource.com.

www.ingramcontent.com/pod-product-compliance
Lightning Source LLC
LaVergne TN
LVHW051510070426
835507LV00022B/3025